MCO P5215.17

THE MARINE CORPS TECHNICAL PUBLICATIONS SYSTEM

I0415714

U.S. MARINE CORPS

PCN 102 075902 00

MCO P5215.17C
PSD
20 Jun 96

MARINE CORPS ORDER P5215.17C

From: Commandant of the Marine Corps
To: Distribution List

Subj: THE MARINE CORPS TECHNICAL PUBLICATIONS SYSTEM

Ref: (a) DoD Instruction 5000.2
      (b) SECNAVINST 5000.2A

Encl: (1) LOCATOR SHEET

1. <u>Purpose</u>. To implement the references and to publish the policies and standards for the operation and maintenance of the Marine Corps Technical Publications System, including the Federal Catalog System publications.

2. <u>Cancellation</u>. MCO P5215.17B.

3. <u>Information</u>. Appendix A lists acronyms used in this Manual.

4. <u>Background</u>. The Marine Corps Technical Publications System was placed in effect in 1961 to provide an uniform method of issuing and maintaining the technical publications within the Marine Corps.

5. <u>Summary of Revision</u>. This Manual has been revised to incorporate organizational changes, to update policies and procedures for acquiring digitized TM's, and to provide information on distribution of publications. This revision should be completely reviewed.

6. <u>Recommendation</u>. Recommendations concerning the contents of the Marine Corps Technical Publications System are invited. Such recommendations will be forwarded to the Commander, Marine Corps Systems Command (PSD) via the appropriate chain of command.

7. <u>Reserve Applicability</u>. This Manual is applicable to the Marine Corps Reserve.

DISTRIBUTION STATEMENT A: Approved for public release; distribution is unlimited.

MCO P5215.17C
20 Jun 96

8. <u>Certification</u>. Reviewed and approved this date.

C. A. MUTTER
By direction

DISTRIBUTION: PCN 10207590200

    Copy to: 7000110 (55)
              7000093/8145005 (2)
              7000099, 144/8145001 (1)

2

LOCATOR SHEET

Subj: THE MARINE CORPS TECHNICAL PUBLICATIONS SYSTEM

Location: _____
           (Indicate location(s) of copy(ies) of this Manual.)

ENCLOSURE (1)

THE MARINE CORPS TECHNICAL PUBLICATIONS SYSTEM

RECORD OF CHANGES

Log completed change action as indicated.

Change Number	Date of Change	Date Entered	Signature of Person Incorporated Change

THE MARINE CORPS TECHNICAL PUBLICATIONS SYSTEM

CONTENTS

THE MARINE CORPS TECHNICAL PUBLICATIONS SYSTEM

CHAPTER 1

TM MANAGEMENT

CHAPTER 1

TM MANAGEMENT

1000. GENERAL INFORMATION. This Manual implements DoDI 5000.2
and SECNAVINST 5000.2A within the Marine Corps and provides
policies, procedures, and delineation of responsibilities for the
acquisition, management, and maintenance of TM's for Marine Corps
systems and equipment.

1001. SCOPE. This Manual is applicable to Headquarters Marine
Corps staff offices, commands, and field activities responsible
for management, acquisition, or maintenance of TM's. The provisions herein apply specifically to TM's, including SL's and
instructional-type publications (e.g., modification/technical
instructions), for equipments/weapons systems. Management level
personnel must recognize the essential relationships of the TM
Management Program with other Marine Corps programs, such as
configuration management, integrated logistics support, and other
materiel management and maintenance systems, to ensure that TM
planning will be coordinated accordingly.

1002. RESPONSIBILITIES

1. The responsibilities for ensuring that the provisions of this
Manual are effected in the administration of the Marine Corps
Technical Publications System are vested in the Commander,
MARCORSYSCOM (PSD). They shall include:

    a. Central management of Marine Corps technical publi-
cations.

    b. In conjunction with MARCORSYSCOM Program Managers, the
acquisition, development of TMCR and CDRL, approval, and promulgation of TM's for Marine Corps equipment.

    c. Establishment of policy and promulgation of formal plans,
procedures, and directives to ensure that the total TM management
program within the Marine Corps is effectively carried out and
implemented.

    d. Review and approval of consolidated Marine Corps comments
on draft and final manuals.

    e. Sponsorship for all Marine Corps TM's.

    f. Establishment of a TM Council to support central manage-
ment.

g. Assisting the program managers in the determination of distribution for all types of technical publications.

h. Providing budget guidance to:

(1) The MARCORSYSCOM Program Managers to assist in their POM for acquisition, review, verification, and update of TM's as required.

(2) MARCORLOGBASES, Albany for anticipated printing costs for new manuals and procurement of other-service TM's.

i. Maintenance of the technical publications portion of the MCPDS, to include:

(1) Assigning PCN's to all technical publications developed, procured, or used by the Marine Corps.

(2) Creating and maintaining currency of all technical publication records in MCPDS.

j. Consolidation and review of all comments on TM's and forwarding to the appropriate TM developer.

k. Preparation and signature of the TM promulgation page including the TM date (TM date shall be the last working day of the month in which the promulgation page was signed).

2. <u>MARCORSYSCOM Program Managers</u>

a. Forward, as applicable, Marine Corps comments on draft and final manuals to MARCORSYSCOM (PSD) for consolidation.

b. Budget and fund for acquisition of new TM's, updates of TM's resulting from ECP's, and for TAD for Marines and civilians participating in TM IPR's, ILSMT meetings, and TM verification.

c. Provide distribution requirements and logistics documentation (i.e., ULSS/LRFS/ILSP) for new TM's to MARCORSYSCOM (PSD).

3. <u>COMMARCORLOGBASES</u>

a. Implement the provisions of this Manual incident to the development and management of technical publications under its cognizance. This responsibility includes preparation, signature, and issuance of the following:

(1) SL publications (input from MARCORSYSCOM required on new and revised SL-3's).

(2) Technical instruction-type publications; i.e., LI, MI, TI, and SI.

(3) Changes and/or revisions to TM's for fielded equipment.

(4) User's Manuals.

b. Provide members to the Marine Corps TM Council.

c. Participate in the review of draft manuals for new equipment; attend IPR's during the development of new or revised manuals.

d. Identify equipment for which depot standards do not exist; subsequently, budget and fund for development of depot maintenance manuals as required for fielded equipment.

e. Budget and fund for the review and TAD associated with new equipment depot manuals.

f. Provide participants for verification efforts on newly-developed TM's. (Equipment Specialist for expertise relative to LSA and SMR codes with maintenance tasks.)

g. Budget and fund for the printing, reproduction, or procurement of other-service publications, and for distribution of all technical publications as designated by MARCORSYSCOM (PSD) to be used by the Marine Corps.

4. <u>COMMARFORLANT and COMMARFORPAC</u>

a. Provide a member for Marine Corps TM Council.

b. Participate in verification of TM's by providing target users to perform hands-on verification as requested by MARCORSYSCOM.

5. Marine Corps Schools and Test Activities. Participate in review/evaluation of draft TM's and assist in TM verification effort.

6. All commanding officers, officers-in-charge, and heads of departments and units shall ensure that:

a. Authorized publications are on hand in the minimum quantity required for efficient operation of their activities.

b. Internal distribution is made.

c. Publications are maintained up to date as changes and/or revisions are promulgated.

d. Prompt action is taken to request decreases or increases in allowances when requirements change.

e. A publications control point is established which will be responsible to:

(1) Review prepared publications.

(2) Ensure that publications are maintained for all equipment their respective commands use or for which they are responsible. Pertinent publications must be readily available to the user where the equipment and material are maintained. Commands are authorized to maintain filler sheets for command files only in the case of multi-volume TM's.

f. Identify deficiencies in publications and notify appropriate publications sponsor by submission of NAVMC 10772 (Recommended Changes to Publications/Logistics-Maintenance Data Coding). The NAVMC 10772 shall be submitted to the COMMARCORLOGBASES (Code 853), 814 Radford Boulevard, Albany, GA 31704-1128 in all cases except when the authentication sheet in the technical publication directs otherwise. Recommended changes may be submitted electronically to the following MARCORLOGBASES, Albany address: Logistics Data Maintenance Branch MB@ILS853@MCLB Albany.

1003. POLICIES. The following policies apply for Marine Corps implementation.

1. Cost. All levels of TM management shall give due emphasis to minimizing the cost requirements of TM's. TM costs shall not duplicate other contractor charges associated with basic engineering data and LSA.

2. Planning

a. The TM acquiring office must develop a TM plan for support of each Marine Corps acquisition to include specific requirements for TM's, including the applicable specifications, users' needs, quantities necessary, printing arrangements, total distribution, and estimated cost. If possible, this plan shall be developed as early as the demonstration and validation phase.

b. Acquisition schedule planning must allow for all phases of TM preparation, validation, verification, changes, production or procurement of preliminary and final copies, and distribution to the users, as required. During the engineering and manufacturing development phase, special consideration should be given to the availability of TM's in preliminary form for operational testing and overpack and for use in advance training of personnel. Refer to appendix B for detailed instructions.

    c. The TM acquisition plan and the TMCR exhibit in the contract must provide for adequate quality assurance procedures, including validation by the contractor and verification by cognizant Marine Corps technical/engineering personnel and target users. The validation and verification processes must include the complete or partial testing or inspection of the information in the TM's against the hardware or basic technical data to ensure its accuracy and adequacy. Appendix C provides definitions, methods, and responsibilities for validation and verification of TM's.

3. <u>Criteria for Acceptable TM's.</u> A TM must reflect the maintenance concept and configuration of the hardware it supports. The TM must be timely and must parallel all approved engineering changes throughout the life cycle of the associated equipment/ weapon systems.

4. <u>Comprehensibility</u>. The TM's must be geared to their users. Accordingly, precise user requirements for technical documentation must be firmly ascertained during the development phase to ensure that each principal user will receive and comprehend the technical information needed to fully accomplish the assigned tasks.

5. <u>Specifications and Standards.</u> The issuance of the Secretary of Defense and the Assistant Secretary of the Navy (RD&A) memoranda setting forth guidance related to acquisition reform, necessitates a change in the use of MIL-SPEC's and MIL-STD's. The use of military specifications and standards and other government documents will be on an exception basis only. When the procuring agency determines that only a MIL-SPEC or MIL-STD will provide the necessary documentation, a request for a waiver, with justification, will be provided as part of the program documentation for approval. Commercial specifications will be used in all possible instances when acquiring technical publications; an alternative method for TM requirements, without the use of MIL-SPEC's or MIL-STD's, could be to define all requirements in the TMCR.

6. <u>Configuration Control</u>. Procedures shall be established to apply configuration control to TM's to ensure that timely issuance of changes and revisions to TM's reflect engineering changes, that new instructions resulting from equipment and system modifications are issued concurrently, and that repair parts lists are updated.

7. Acquisitions of TM's

    a. Military TM's. TM's shall be purchased by a separate, priced contract line item. Each contract line item shall reference a separate exhibit which identifies the TM's being acquired. The exhibit shall be the TMCR, attached to the CDRL (DD Form 1423). Refer to appendix D for procedural instructions and sample TMCR. Acquisition of program or administrative data, such as plans, reports, and schedules, requires a DID listed on a CDRL (DD Form 1423) as a separate exhibit. All TMCR's and CDRL's shall have the signature approval of MARCORSYSCOM (PSD).

    b. Commercial. The TMCR is not required for procurement of commercial manuals; the requirement for commercial manuals shall be described in the SOW. DID's are applicable in this case.

8. Deliverables. A TM master (camera-ready copy) shall be acquired by the government for all technical publications except commercial manuals. In addition, the requirement for digitized data shall be included in the engineering and manufacturing development phase TMCR. Digital data shall be a deliverable on all production contracts. Refer to appendix B for detailed information.

9. Funding

    a. TM development for new, modified, or product-improved equipment will be funded by the appropriation which funds the hardware and will be procured on the hardware contracts as separate line items. Costs for updating TM documentation of a hardware change shall be considered as essential parts of the hardware change costs. Final cost data should be compared with cost estimates, as furnished on DD Forms 633-2 (Contract Pricing Proposal (Technical Publications)) validated, and recorded as integral phases of effective TM management.

    b. The program manager, or project officer, as the case may be, shall budget and fund for TAD for civilian and military personnel who are required to travel in support of his programs, meetings, and verification efforts.

    c. COMMARCORLOGBASES shall budget and fund for the development of depot maintenance manuals for fielded equipment when required.

10. Commercial Manuals. The maximum use of commercial TM's is encouraged; however, it is essential that all proposed commercial TM's be evaluated by the program manager in conjunction with MARCORSYSCOM (PSD) to ensure that:

a. Commercial manuals reflect the configuration of the hardware.

b. Technical contents are adequate for Marine Corps operation and maintenance of the hardware, or can be made adequate by limited supplementation. A commercial manual is rejected if it requires more than 15 percent rewrite and a new manual may be required of the contractor. (A contract modification may be required to effect this requirement.)

c. Marine Corps TM identification numbers and PCN's are assigned to commercial manuals, when possible.

d. Copyright is released to the government to allow reprint of the manual.

e. Commercial manuals contain parts lists and illustrations which accurately support Marine Corps provisioning.

NOTE: A commercial manual which contains a parts list will not be duplicated by issuance of an SL-4. A Marine Corps change may be issued to provide or clarify information, if required.

11. Cross-Service Agreements. Cross-service agreements shall be extended, when feasible, to the other military services and DLA. When the Marine Corps is the procuring activity, the other military services and DLA shall be interrogated, especially when a commonality of hardware is anticipated, to determine whether a proposed or existing TM for the hardware is under procurement or currently available. As a corollary to this, the Marine Corps shall receive and respond to interrogations from the other military services and DLA relative to proposed or existing Marine Corps TM's.

12. Other Service Manuals. In lieu of development of Marine Corps-unique manuals, manuals developed by a DoD agency, other service, or a commercial activity will be adopted whenever possible. These documents will be identified, modified as necessary, and acquired during the acquisition process. Separate or stand-alone components lists and repair parts lists will not be developed by the Marine Corps when other service manuals are procured for support of the end item being fielded. A Marine Corps change to the manuals may be issued to incorporate any unique changes required.

NOTE: Depot Maintenance manuals required for previously fielded equipment will not be developed until it is ascertained that the requirement cannot be satisfied by a manual already in existence or under development.

13. <u>Training Compatibility</u>. The TM's shall serve as the basic source of technical information for equipments/weapons systems training. Although trainee workbooks, instructor guides, skill descriptions, and other instructional material may be developed for effective training operations, positive management action shall be exercised to prevent the procurement of the same information, as separate items, for both TM's and training courses. The importance of parallel effort between TM development and training cannot be over-emphasized. Coordination between TM and training personnel during acquisition planning is essential. Marine Corps schools should be directly involved in TM development by participating in IPR's to ensure that the schools' training requirements are satisfied. Validated TM's must be available for instructor/key personnel training.

14. <u>LSA</u>. When LSA is invoked in contracts, the LSA data generated therein shall be used to the maximum extent to define and develop the source data for the TM's. In addition, LSA-045 and LSA-034 Reports shall be used to ensure that Components Lists (SL-3) and Repair Parts Lists (SL-4) can be verified concurrently with the operation and maintenance manuals and fielded in conjunction with the manuals. Appropriate LSAR files with data elements identified shall be invoked in contracts to avoid duplication of effort and cost in preparation of SL-3's and SL-4's.

15. <u>Metric Measurement</u>. The use of metric measurement in the preparation of TM's will be determined by the type of measurement used for design of the system/equipment. When metric measurement is used in TM's, a metric conversion chart shall be included in the manual or, if the requirement can be identified in time to include in contract, standard equivalents will be included in parentheses after the metric measurement.

16. <u>Digital Data</u>. Digital data is required for the life cycle management of technical publications. Program managers shall require the delivery of digital data per appendix B. Detail requirements for the type and delivery of digital data will be described in the TMCR. MARCORSYSCOM (PSD) will provide guidance to the program manager for the acquisition of digital data.

17. <u>IETM and ETM</u>. Definitions and types of IETM's and ETM's are in appendix E. Every effort should be made to procure IETM's or ETM's for weapon systems/equipment. Class 3, 4, and 5 ETM/IETM are the most beneficial types for life cycle management of the data because of its editable format. MARCORSYSCOM (PSD) will make recommendations to the program manager for the type of ETM/IETM to support the weapon system/equipment. ETM/IETM data procured must be compatible with the government furnished software.

18. <u>Government Furnished Software</u>: IADS. Every effort shall be made to use the government furnished software. IADS is a Micro-Soft Windows application that is government owned. IADS is capable of running on any computer that meets the minimum requirements of a 80386 PC with 8 megabytes of RAM. IADS can be furnished to defense contractors upon request from:

    Commander USAMICOM
    ATTN: AMSMI-MMC-LS-SA
    Redstone Arsenal, AL 35898-5238
    DSN 746-4024

    a. IADS uses SGML, (ISO 879 SGML and MIL-M-28001) as the internal file format for textual data. Both Vector and Raster graphics are supported through the CALS standard data formats, MIL-D-28003 CGM, and MIL-R-28002 Raster Type I, as well as other industry standard formats. IADS documents can be presented on screen in full color or black and white with support for multiple fonts.

    b. IADS is divided into two separate applications, READER and AUTHOR.

        (1) The Reader software is designed to display the final document to the end-user. The user will have the ability to view documents and navigate through them to find needed information with some control over the display area. The user can access menus, button commands, "hotspots," or hypertext links by using the mouse or keyboard inputs. The user can also utilize the search feature to locate information. Special user tools include User Defined Private and Public Notes, Bookmarks, Reports, and Print capability from the IADS Reader and both ViewImage and ZoomView, the image viewing tools. The user also has access to a complete Online Help document for assistance while using the IADS Reader.

        (2) The IADS Author application provides tools to aid in hypertext document creation. IADS Author allows the document creator to test the document with the same functions and tools that the user has available with the IADS Reader. The author can compose a document either in IADS or in another text editor by utilizing SGML tags and attributes.

    c. <u>IADS Software User's Manual</u>. In-depth information and details can be found in the current version of the Software User's Manual that can also be obtained through USAMICOM.

19. <u>Contractor Furnished Data</u>. Contractor developed or commercial software used to develop ETM's or IETM's shall be compatible with the IADS Reader. The contractor/commercial delivered

digital data must be editable/reviveable in the IADS
Author/Reader/RPSTL.

CHAPTER 2

TYPES OF TECHNICAL PUBLICATIONS

CHAPTER 2

TYPES OF TECHNICAL PUBLICATIONS

2000. DEFINITIONS. Technical publications are official documents used by the Marine Corps which support materiel and equipment. Types include:

1. TM. A TM normally contains a description of the equipment,
illustrated parts breakdown, and instructions for:

   a. Initial preparation for use (i.e., installation).

   b. Theory of operation.

   c. Operation.

   d. Troubleshooting.

   e. Maintenance.

   f. Overhaul.

   g. Lubrication.

   h. IROAN. That maintenance technique which determines the
minimum repairs necessary to restore equipment, components, or
assemblies to prescribed maintenance serviceability standards by
using all available diagnostic equipment and test procedures and
by minimizing disassembly and parts replacement. These procedures will place the system in good-to-excellent operating capability (condition code A). Refer to appendix F for guidance/
additional information.

   i. Related technical information or procedures (other than
administrative).

   j. A TM also provides information on collection-type items,
with components, including the collateral materiel required to
make the item combat-operative, listed under both supply system
responsibility and using unit responsibility. (These instructions constitute a list which may be referenced in a major list
when the subordinate components are used with a major end item.
For example, a components list for a receiver/transmitter shall
be cited in a TM for a communications shelter to eliminate the
necessity for relisting all components of the subordinate item.
Quantities listed in the TM or SL-3 represent the quantity for
that major end item only; reference only should be made to the
T/E for allowances.)

k. Repair parts list which furnishes information on repair parts required for maintenance and support of the equipment. It also reflects nonsupply item for information purposes.

2. TI. A TI provides:

a. Professional techniques and maintenance procedures.

b. Interim/supplementary technical information that later will be incorporated into a permanent technical publication.

c. Precautions concerning technical problems and identification of the instructions to be published to correct them.

d. Administrative technical details (primarily concerning equipment maintenance) which can be more suitably disseminated by an instruction than by another type of publication. (Examples are applicable forms to be used, special safety measures, serviceability standards, etc.)

e. Testing and inspection procedures.

NOTE: A TI does not normally require the use of parts, special tools, or kits, other than test kits.

3. MI. An MI provides instructions for uniformly modifying equipment to correct deficiencies in equipment design and to add tactical and technical advantages. An MI's importance in materiel management requires that it be recorded by the equipment's serial number, if possible. An MI includes any instruction which meets the criteria of:

a. Urgency.

b. Indispensability to an item or to a system's operation or effectiveness.

c. Inclusion of guidance on the use of kits or parts.

4. LI. An LI, also identified as an LO, prescribes lubrication instructions for equipment, describes proper lubricants, establishes required intervals, and explains lubrication maintenance.

5. SI. An SI furnishes supply information on equipment acquisition, regulation, and availability. It explains technical aspects of supply matters but does not provide administrative instructions. The SI's in the 5600 series are issued quarterly to cancel MI's, TI's, LI's, and other SI's.

NOTE: MI's, TI's, and SI's may be cited as authority for requisitioning parts needed to complete equipment modification or for requisitioning repair or replacement parts, until changes can be made to the appropriate TM's.

6. SC. An SC provides information for logistics support of specific items, equipment, or weapons systems. It is normally a planning document explaining operation, maintenance, and equipment capabilities.

7. ULSS. A ULSS advises the FMF and other selected commands of the plan to field and logistically support new items of equipment or systems being procured by the Marine Corps.

8. RS. RS information and IROAN and depot maintenance repair procedures will henceforth be incorporated into one manual and titled "Depot Maintenance Manual." Depot maintenance manuals will be developed for all previously-fielded Marine Corps equipment for which depot maintenance is required and for which equipment manuals were not in a 15&P format. The depot maintenance manual shall provide all maintenance, overhaul, and IROAN procedures required for fifth echelon. Stand alone IROAN standards will be developed when an approved rebuild standard is already in existence. IROAN standards will be appendices to the rebuild standards.

9. FT. An FT provides, in tabular or chart form, the data needed for firing a weapon accurately on a target under both standard and adverse climatic and environmental conditions.

10. Supplement. A supplement is a subsidiary document which complements/augments information contained in a technical publication, primarily a TM.

11. Letter Changes. Letter changes to other military service and commercial publications (e.g., change A, change B, etc.) reflect Marine Corps-peculiar supply information that takes precedence over data originally listed in the publications and are used per instructions contained in the changes. Cross-reference lists and SMR codes are normally issued in these changes to supplement or provide Marine Corps-peculiar data. They also change technical procedures when the Marine Corps configuration is different from other services.

12. Publication Index MCPDS/SL-1-2. MCPDS shall be the primary index of authorized publications required for equipment support. MCPDS is an on-line system that is updated daily. Marine Corps activities shall use MCPDS for proper identification of publications requisitioned from the publications stock point per instructions contained in the current edition of MCO P5600.31. Marine Corps activities without access to MCPDS may use the microfiche index SL-1-2 as a secondary source of authorized

publications for equipment support. The SL-1-2 is updated
quarterly and is sponsored by MARCORLOGBASES, Albany.

   a. Part I - Cross-Reference List of Equipments to ID Numbers. End items, major components, and collection type items are
listed in alphabetical sequence with their assigned ID numbers to
provide a cross-reference to part II. Equipment is identified by
Federal item name, technical name, trade or colloquial name,
type, or model number.

   b. Part II - Cross-Reference List of Equipments to Maintenance Publications. This part is arranged in number sequence
as a major entry on the line with the name of the equipment.
Indented under the ID number are sequential prefix/control
numbers of supporting publications. The publication number is
indented under the equipment name. Change numbers are listed by
prefix/control number and publication number, indented under the
publication title with the date of the change in the date column.

   c. Part III - Index of Superseded or Rescinded Publications. This part lists superseded, rescinded, obsolete,
canceled, and deleted publications in prefix/control number
sequence, with the publication title or number, and the date.
When a publication has been superseded, the prefix/control
number, title or number, and date of the new publication are
shown. Part III also shows whether selected changes or the basic
publication and all changes are included in the supersession or
rescission. An asterisk (*) preceding an entry in this index
indicates a new or change action not previously published.

13. SL. SL's provide all levels of Marine Corps supply and
maintenance operations with essential, up-to-date supply information. For all Marine Corps-managed supply items, including
principal items, major components, assemblies, modification kits,
and repair parts, these publications provide NSN, Federal item
names, Federal item descriptions, reference part numbers,
illustrations, unit of issue, ID numbers, stock level guidance
data, cross-references, and other related data. These publications are tailored specifically to the supply requirements of
Marine Corps users. They list only items for which Marine Corps
user interest is registered in the centrally controlled DoD
record maintained by the DLSC. The DLSC is a DLA field activity
designated the central control and monitoring point for the
Federal Catalog System.

14. Types of SL's. SL publications include:

   a. Publications Index (SL-1-2). The SL-1-2 is an index of
publications required for equipment support. It contains a
cross-reference list of equipments to ID numbers, a

cross-reference list of equipments to maintenance publications, and an index of superseded or rescinded publications.

b. <u>Publications Stocked by the Marine Corps (SL-1-3)</u>. This is a microfiche listing of all types of technical publications authorized for use by the Marine Corps which are stocked at the MARCORLOGBASES, Albany. Publications prepared by other DoD activities that have been adopted and/or authorized for use by the Marine Corps are included. This index is used by all echelons of command to determine if the publications required to accomplish the assigned mission of the organization concerned are stocked. Commands shall requisition and maintain those publications required. The index is updated quarterly and is sponsored by MARCORLOGBASES, Albany.

c. <u>Components List (SL-3)</u>. An SL-3 contains illustrations, technical data, and item identification data on collateral and collection-type items within the Marine Corps. It lists all components for the collection-type supply items, such as major combinations, systems, vehicles, groups, outfits, sets, or assortments. Collateral material that is required to complete an end item is also identified. When the SL-3 is incorporated into the basic TM, the manual front cover will be designated as "With Components List." The current edition of MCO P4400.150 contains a complete description of the categories of SL-3 components.

d. <u>Repair Parts List (SL-4)</u>. An SL-4 lists repair parts and provides illustrations for each end item, component, or major assembly requiring maintenance and supply support. It provides the supply and maintenance information for identification of repair parts required to support Marine Corps equipment. Through the repair parts list, the technician, the mechanic, and the repairer are linked to the supply system. When the SL-4 is an integrated part of the basic TM, the manual will be designated as "&P." If separated from the basic manual when procured, it will be designated "P."

NOTE: The MARCORSYSCOM, in an effort to reduce the quantity of different technical manuals (TM, SL-3, and SL-4) used by the FMF has been procuring technical manuals in a TM-10 W/components (SL-3) and TM 25&P or 24&P format for new acquisitions of fielded equipment. This policy of consolidating SL's into TM's whenever possible shall also apply to manuals procured or updated during reprocurement of equipment.

e. <u>AL's for End Items and Components</u>

(1) The AL (SL-6-1) is a computer output microfiche which contains a cross-reference of all centrally managed end items, major components, fifth echelon secondary depot

reparables, and modification kits maintained in the computer for system management with assigned, changed, or deleted ID numbers. There are three sections that are a cross-reference between current ID numbers, NSN's, item name, model or type number, and TAM numbers. It is used in supply management to identify end item, major components, fifth echelon depot reparable items, and modification kits. The AL is a MARCORLOGBASES, Albany sponsored publication and is updated quarterly.

(2) The AL (SL-6-2) is a reference document used to identify repair parts application for use in supply management. Repair parts are listed in NSN sequence. It is a computer output microfiche which shows the ID number of each end item, major component, depot reparable item, or modification kit beneath the NSN to show the application of the NSN.

f. Special List (SL-8). SL-8's contain items which are functionally the same and are grouped together for convenience at all levels. They contain reference stock numbers, item names and descriptions, and other supply management information pertinent to supply items which are grouped together for management and requisitioning purposes (e.g., tariff sizes, chemical defense items, rifle team equipment, blank forms, etc.). SL-8's are used as a convenient reference source of information on special groups of items.

15. FEDLOG Data. FEDLOG data consists of item/colloquial name index, NSN's, CAGE data, I&S, characteristics information, reference number data, management data, and freight data. FEDLOG also contains service-unique information. FEDLOG, sponsored and prepared by DLA, is distributed on CD-ROM by MARCORLOGBASES, Albany.

THE MARINE CORPS TECHNICAL PUBLICATIONS SYSTEM

CHAPTER 3

TECHNICAL PUBLICATION PRESENTATION, NUMBERING, AND CONTENT

CHAPTER 3

TECHNICAL PUBLICATION PRESENTATION, NUMBERING, AND CONTENT

3000. **TECHNICAL PUBLICATION PRESENTATION**. Information presented in technical publications requires that it be separated into units for dissemination to the field.

1. Single Unit-Technical Publication. The single-unit technical publication (manual) has complete information on the equipment to which it pertains. For example, a single-unit TM may contain information from operator's (first echelon) instructions through depot (fifth echelon) maintenance procedures on an item of equipment. The single-unit publication is generally one volume and is adaptable to both general technical subjects and equipment. However, if a single unit publication is too large, it will be divided into volumes. In such cases, each publication cover will clearly show the volume number and how many volumes pertain.

2. Multiple-Unit Technical Publication. The multiple-unit technical publication is normally used to disseminate information on highly complicated equipment or systems consisting of several components per the echelons of maintenance. Essential instructions are published in what constitutes an interrelated set or series of publications having a common basic identification number. This separation of instructions facilitates their application by personnel at different organizational levels who have various functional responsibilities. It also minimizes publications of cumbersome size and prevents the unnecessary dissemination of data to disinterested or unqualified personnel. Thus, for example, a multiple-unit technical publication may, as a set or series, constitute a components list (SL-3) and the repair parts (SL-4), operator's (first echelon) manual, an organizational (second echelon) maintenance manual, and a field through depot (third through fifth echelons) maintenance manual. The multiple-unit publication may also be divided into volumes if it is too large. Each volume will show the volume number and number of volumes involved.

3001. **NUMBERING SYSTEM.** The number assigned to a technical publication may consist of as many as five elements. (Refer to figure 3-1.)

1. Type of Publication (Abbreviated). The two- or three-letter abbreviation indicates the type of publication; e.g., TM, MI, TI, etc.

2. Basic Number. One of three numbers is assigned in the following order of preference:

a. ID Number. The equipment ID number, consisting of five digits suffixed by a letter of the alphabet (excluding O and I) is assigned to a system, major item, or multiple-use major components. If the publication covers more than one model of the same equipment, the suffix letter is dropped and specific models are listed on the manual cover.

b. FSC Number. The four-digit FSC number assigned to the materiel is based on the group and class of materiel rather than on the ID number; e.g., 6115, 6665.

c. SSIC. The four-or five-digit SSIC is used when the publication provides general information on a wide range of equipment (e.g., electronics, motor transport, etc.); SSIC's are selected from the current edition of SECNAVINST 5210.11.

3. Maintenance Echelon Number. The echelon-of-maintenance indicator is a significant information number provided to show who is responsible for performing the maintenance tasks.

a. -10. First echelon only (operator or crew).

b. -20. Second echelon only (general support) (organizational maintenance).

c. -30. Third echelon only (direct support (intermediate) maintenance).

d. -40. Fourth echelon only (general maintenance support (intermediate) maintenance).

e. -50. Fifth echelon only (depot maintenance).

f. Any combination of these echelons to which a publication would apply:

(1) -12. First and second echelons.

(2) -13. First through third echelons.

(3) -14. First through fourth echelons.

(4) -15. First through fifth echelons.

(5) -23. Second and third echelons.

(6) -24. Second through fourth echelons.

(7) -25. Second through fifth echelons.

(8) -34. Third and fourth echelons.

(9) -<u>35</u>. Third through fifth echelons.

(10) -<u>45</u>. Fourth and fifth echelons.

4. <u>Parts List Designation</u>. The letter "P" will follow the maintenance indicator number if the manual is a parts list, i.e.,
-24P, -34P, etc. When a parts list is incorporated into a manual
with text, the TM shall be designated "-##&P", as applicable.

5. <u>Sequence Number</u>. The sequence number follows the basic number or maintenance echelon indicator, as appropriate. The maintenance echelon indicator is not considered as part of the number
when assigning the sequence number. A virgule (/) separates the
sequence number from the preceding element. The sequence number
indicates a manual as being one of a series for a specific piece
of equipment.

6. <u>Edition Designator.</u> The edition designator, if applicable,
is an alphabetic character, starting with capital suffix "A,"
that indicates each revision of a technical publication after its
initial printing. The edition designator appears as the last
element of the total identification number; thus, it immediately
follows the maintenance echelon number or sequence number, as
appropriate.

3002. <u>STANDARD CONTENTS</u>. Standard contents for TM's include a
cover, authentication-distribution page, record of change page,
table of contents, list of illustrations and tables, and technical contents. Guidance for standard contents for instruction-
type publications is covered in the current edition of
MIL-P-28999. The manual date (last working day of the month)
shall be placed on the promulgation page and the List of
Effective Pages.

3003. <u>PCN</u>. The PCN is an eleven digit number assigned to a
publication to denote distribution and serve as a stock number
for requisitioning purposes. See appendix G for distribution.

1. <u>PCN Assignment</u>. HQMC (ARD) assigns PCN's for non-technical
publications and MARCORSYSCOM (PSD) assigns PCN's for technical
publications. The first three digits of a PCN (referred to as a
PCN prefix) are listed in appendix C of NAVMC 2761 (Catalog of
Publications). The next five digits are assigned using ID, SSIC,
or FSC, whichever applies. The ninth digit is assigned for
internal use by MARCORSYSCOM (PSD). The last two digits are
assigned designating basic/change/supplement/errata/etc. as
follows:

MARINE CORPS MANUALS

Basic	00
Change 001	01
Change A	50
Binders	60
Supplements	70
Errata	80
Interim Change	90

ARMY MANUALS

Erratum	10
MC Change to Army Publication	50
Addendum	60
Supplements	70

2. SL-3, MI, TI, and SI. When the publication is applicable to several weapon systems, the FSC shall be used as the publication identification number (e.g., SL-3-6110/1). Individual NSN, model number, and ID numbers are listed below the Marine Corps Seal on the cover. If the NSN's, model numbers, and ID numbers are too numerous to fit on the cover below the Marine Corps Seal, the seal may not be used.

THE MARINE CORPS TECHNICAL PUBLICATIONS SYSTEM

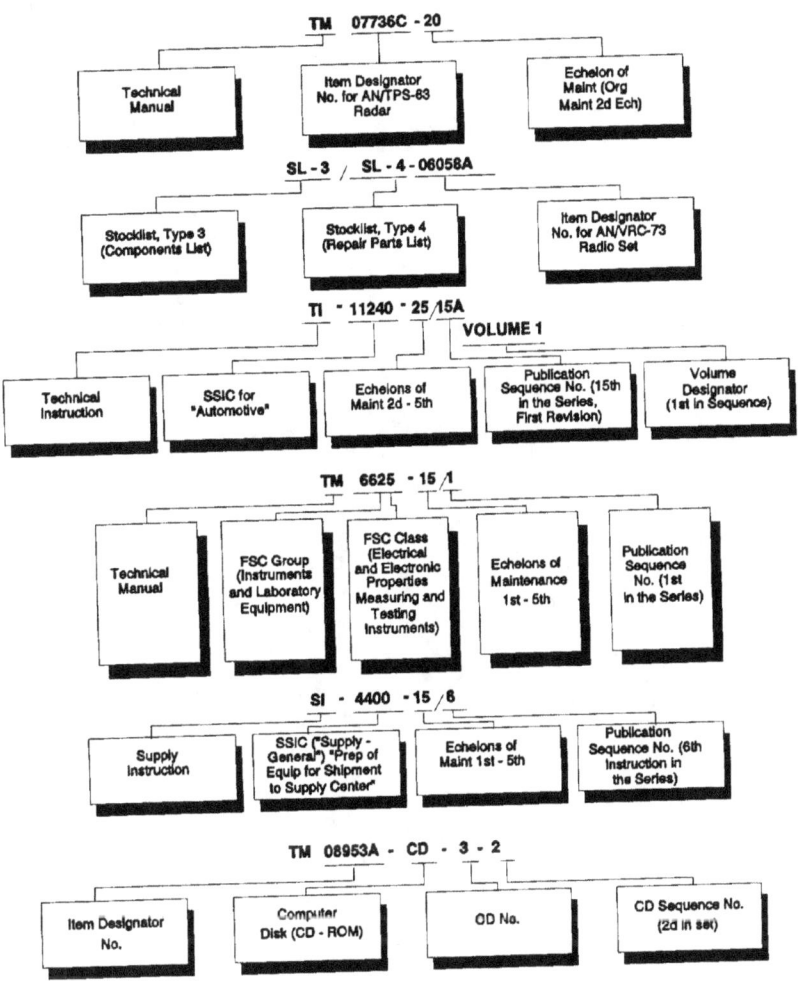

Figure 3-1.--Example of Numbering System.

THE MARINE CORPS TECHNICAL PUBLICATIONS SYSTEM

CHAPTER 4

PRINTING AND REVISION

CHAPTER 4

PRINTING AND REVISION

4000. <u>PRINTING PROCEDURES</u>. Technical publications are printed per the current edition of MCO P5600.31.

4001. <u>SIZE AND BINDING</u>. The size and binding of technical publications are determined by the TMCR. Normally, technical publications are printed on standard size sheets, 8 1/2 by 11 inches trimmed (image area will not exceed 7 1/4 x 9 inches), and are produced as three-hole-punched looseleaf publications.

4002. <u>CHANGES</u>. Technical publications are kept current by changes issued as:

1. <u>Pen Changes</u>. Minor corrections, limited to changes which can be clearly and easily annotated, are transmitted as pen changes. Insertion of new paragraph(s) will not be considered a minor change. New page replacements are recommended in all cases.

2. <u>Page Inserts</u>. Extensive changes are incorporated into the basic publication as new page inserts. These page inserts are transmitted with instructions for replacing the pages. The transmittal page, directing a change to the basic manual/publication, shall be filed behind the promulgation page with the most recent transmittal page on top.

4003. <u>REPRINT POLICY.</u> Reprints of publications include all effective change pages. A "note" on the cover of the publication shows the changes included in the publication; e.g., "This reprint includes Changes 1, 2, 3, etc." Reprint for stock replenishment shall not take precedence over new Marine Corps manuals.

4004. <u>REVISION POLICY</u>. It is the responsibility of the sponsor of a technical publication to review it annually for essentiality, currency, and accuracy, and to plan for the necessary page inserts, pen changes, or revision. A publication will be revised when 25 percent or more of its original contents have changed. A publication is rescinded when it has served its purpose. The publication is superseded in whole or in part by a new publication, special instructions, or by deleting it from the Index of Publications Authorized and Stocked, Marine Corps SL-1-2, SL-1-3, and MCPDS.

THE MARINE CORPS TECHNICAL PUBLICATIONS SYSTEM

CHAPTER 5

OTHER SERVICE PUBLICATIONS AND COMMERCIAL MANUALS

CHAPTER 5

OTHER SERVICE PUBLICATIONS AND COMMERCIAL MANUALS

5000. <u>PUBLICATIONS PREPARED AND PRINTED BY OTHER MILITARY</u>
SERVICES. The Marine Corps shall use other military services'
technical publications to the maximum extent practicable. The
Marine Corps shall bring these publications into its system as
follows:

1. <u>Joint-Service Publications</u>. A joint-service publication is a
single version of a publication coordinated by two or more services. When the Marine Corps participates in the development of
a joint-service publication, the Marine Corps identification
number will be assigned and an authentication sheet shall be
included to show that it has been approved for Marine Corps use.

2. <u>Joint-Service Publication Changes</u>. The following procedures
must be followed for changes to joint-service publications:

    a. <u>Marine Corps is TM sponsor</u>: Draft changes must be coor-
dinated with joint user(s) for concurrence.

    b. <u>TM Sponsor is Another Service</u>: Marine Corps will request
service sponsor publish a change when required.

3. <u>Other Service Publications</u>. Whenever feasible, the Marine
Corps shall procure and use a publication prepared specifically
for another service or other services. Although use of this type
of publication is authorized, the user must understand that,
while it supports equipment, it does not revoke Marine Corps
policy or instructions in Marine Corps publications. If necessary, changes to another service publication shall be issued as
Marine Corps lettered changes (e.g., Change A), numbered supple-
ments (e.g., USMC Supplement No. 1), or as separate TI's to adapt
the publication to the particular needs of the Marine Corps.

5001. <u>COMMERCIAL EQUIPMENT MANUALS</u>. The Marine Corps will make
maximum use of those commercially available manufacturer's
manuals (or modifications thereof) which meet its requirements.

1. The Marine Corps procures numerous items of designed equipment which need little or no modification for Marine Corps use.
The Marine Corps also requires many items of commercial equipment
for which there is low or intermittent use. This type of
equipment does not warrant the high cost of providing repair
parts lists and TM's. For most of this commercial equipment,
commercial manuals are adequate.

2. Commercial manuals will usually be identified by the manufacturer's form or identification numbers; however, a Marine Corps
identification number will be printed on the cover, when at all
possible. Existing specifications require that the manufacturer
of the commercial equipment supplement this manual, as necessary,
to ensure its full applicability to Marine Corps requirements.

3. Should a Marine Corps supplement be required for the parts
lists, technical information, etc., it shall be prepared and
issued per instructions in this Manual.

4. Commercial manuals shall be procured for nondevelopmental
items and supplemented as required.

CHAPTER 6

INFORMATION FEEDBACK

CHAPTER 6

INFORMATION FEEDBACK

6000. <u>INFORMATION SYSTEM FOR PUBLICATIONS FEEDBACK</u>. Technical publications play a critical role in achieving system and equipment readiness. Because of this factor, the currency and accuracy of the data published in these documents are essential. Form NAVMC 10772 provides a medium for accelerating information feedback to MARCORLOGBASES, Albany to effect the necessary corrections, changes, and/or revisions, as appropriate. With the use of Form NAVMC 10772, users at all levels may communicate directly, without staffing, to MARCORLOGBASES, Albany when citing errors and submitting recommendations; however, submission of recommended SMR code changes will be staffed through unit commanders or designated representatives for concurrence. Originator's of NAVMC 10772's must include full name, address, and telephone number to ensure evaluation of and response to their requests. Typographical errors and FSC changes need not be reported.

   NOTE: All NAVMC 10772's should be submitted to MARCORLOGBASES, Albany unless the authentication sheet in a Marine Corps manual directs otherwise. Recommended changes may be submitted electronically to the following MARCORLOGBASES Albany address: Logistics Data Maintenance Branch MB@ILS853@MCLB Albany.

6001. <u>AVAILABILITY OF FORM NAVMC 10772 (RECOMMENDED CHANGES TO TECHNICAL PUBLICATION)</u>. Users of technical publications shall requisition NAVMC 10772's, as necessary, through normal Marine Corps supply channels. Refer to SL-8-09993 for NSN.

6002. <u>USING UNIT ACTION</u>. Units shall obtain and maintain a supply of form NAVMC 10772's for use in reporting deficiencies in TM's (including preliminary TM's), errors, and/or omissions, and for submitting suggestions for improvements and additions in all applications (i.e., test and operation) directly to the COMMARCORLOGBASES (Code 853), 814 Radford Boulevard, Albany, GA 31704-1128.

APPENDIX A

ACRONYMS

AI	Artificial Intelligence
AL	Application List
ASCII	American Standard Code for Information Interchange
ATIS	Advanced Technical Information System
BMP	Bit Map Graphics
CAGE	Commercial and Government Entity
CALS	Continuous Acquisition and Life Cycle Support
CCITT	Consultative Committee on International Telegraphy and Telephone
CD-ROM	Computer Disk-Read Only Memory
CDRL	Contract Data Requirements List
COMMARCORLOGBASES	Commander, Marine Corps Logistics Bases
COMMARFORLANT	Commander, Marine Forces Atlantic
COMMARFORPAC	Commander, Marine Forces Pacific
COTS	Commercial, Off-the-Shelf
DAC	Days After Contract
DID	Data Item Description
DLA	Defense Logistics Agency
DLSC	Defense Logistics Services Center
DoD	Department of Defense
DoDI	Department of Defense Instruction
ECP	Engineering Change Proposal
ETM	Electronic Technical Manual

FAT	First Article Test
FEDLOG	Federal Logistics Data
FMF	Fleet Marine Force
FSC	Federal Supply Class
FT	Firing Table
I&S	Interchangeability and Substitutability
IADS	Interactive Authoring and Display System
ID	Item Designator
IETIS	Interactive Electronic Technical Information System
IETM	Interactive Electronic Technical Manual
ILSMT	Integrated Logistics Support Management Team
ILSP	Integrated Logistics Support Plan
IPR	In-Process Review
IROAN	Inspect and Repair Only As Necessary
ISO	International Standards Organization
LEM	Logistics Element Manager
LI	Lubrication Instruction
LO	Lubrication Order
LRFS	Logistics Requirements and Funding Summary
LSA	Logistics Support Analysis
LSAR	Logistics Support Analysis Record
MARCORLOGBASES	Marine Corps Logistics Bases
MARCORSYSCOM	Marine Corps Systems Command
MARFORLANT	Marine Forces Atlantic
MARFORPAC	Marine Forces Pacific

MC	Marine Corps
MCPDS	Marine Corps Publications Distribution System
MI	Modification Instruction
MIL-SPEC	Military Specification
MIL-STD	Military Standard
NSN	National Stock Number
PCN	Publication Control Number
PMCS	Preventive Maintenance Checks and Services
POM	Program Objectives Memorandum
PSD	Program Support, Technical Documentation Branch
QA	Quality Assurance
R&D	Research and Development
RAM	Random Access Memory
RD&A	Research, Development, and Acquisition
RPSTL	Repair Parts and Special Tool List
RS	Rebuild Standard
SC	Support Concept
SECNAVINST	Secretary of the Navy Instruction
SGML	Standardized General Markup Language
SI	Supply Instruction
SL	Stocklist
SMR	Source Maintenance Recoverability
SOW	Statement of Work
SSIC	Standard Subject Identification Code
T/E	Table of Equipment

TAD	Temporary Additional Duty
TAM	Table of Authorized Materiel
TI	Technical Instruction
TM	Technical Manual
TMCR	Technical Manual Contract Requirements
TMPODS	TM Print on Demand System
ULSS	User's Logistics Support Summary
USAMICOM	U.S. Army Missile Command
WP	Word Processing

APPENDIX B

PROCEDURES FOR ACQUISITION OF TECHNICAL PUBLICATIONS

1. When the need for a TM to support new or modified equipment is recognized, the responsible or acquiring office will review the procurement package and determine what type of manual is required.

2. The type of contract to which the requirement relates is of prime importance. The following milestone phases are defined and discussed below:

   a. <u>Demonstration and Validation</u>. During this acquisition phase, there will be no justification for a complete TM; thus, there is no requirement for camera-ready copy or art work. Simple operation and maintenance instructions to meet criteria for training and service test will be sufficient. Keep in mind that the prototype or service test equipment may not be followed by an engineering and manufacturing development contract.

   b. <u>Engineering and Manufacturing Development</u>. This acquisition phase intensifies the overall effort of testing and must be supportable with complete data. Complete manuals to include troubleshooting, schematics, functional diagrams, theory of operation, and complete repair procedures are a must. The contractor must be required to validate and the government will verify the preliminary TM to ensure accuracy and adequacy for training, development testing, and operational testing. In-process reviews will be conducted to ensure that the contractor is adhering to the contractual requirements and schedules. This preliminary manual will be updated during the production contract and will become the final manual to support the equipment. There will be no requirement for reproducible, camera-ready copy or final artwork; however, digitized data should be procured for major end items.

   c. <u>Production and Deployment</u>. The preliminary manual procured, verified, and tested during engineering and manufacturing development will be updated/revised to incorporate government comments resulting from reviews, IPR's, training, and testing. All new/revised material will be validated and verified prior to acceptance by the government. Camera-ready copy and final artwork are procured as required in this phase of acquisition. Electronic (digital) data shall be updated/procured on all production contracts.

3. The responsible TM office or TM LEM will, after review of all procurement documents, determine the requirement for TM's and

provide the contract exhibit package for incorporation into the procurement document.

4. <u>Contract Exhibits</u>. The contract exhibit shall be a complete package containing the TMCR and CDRL's as required. Refer to appendix C for preparation instructions. The TMCR replaces or negates the need for a SOW and a DID for preparation of TM's. If the procurement work package or request for proposal contains a SOW, use the following:

"Technical Publications. The contractor shall prepare/de-velop/update/revise (as applicable) the TM(s) in accordance with TMCR No. _____."

a. All technical (military) manuals or instructions require a contract exhibit (TMCR); this includes requirements for updated or revised manuals. The TMCR will be referenced on the CDRL. Commercial manuals for nondevelopmental or off-the-shelf equipment do not require a TMCR since they will be described in the SOW.

b. Administrative data such as TM plans, financial reports, status reports, minutes of meetings, and validation and verification certificates shall be called out in the contract on the CDRL Form 1423 and accompanied by the DID.

B-2

THE MARINE CORPS TECHNICAL PUBLICATIONS SYSTEM

APPENDIX C

VALIDATION AND VERIFICATION OF TM'S

1. <u>Validation</u>. Validation is the contractor's responsibility.

    a. The object of validation is to assure that the contractor has expended his best effort to provide accurate and adequate TM content for support of the weapon system per the approved maintenance plan.

    b. Principles of operation, system and component description, source codes, and wiring data and schematics shall be validated against engineering source data. Operating and maintenance procedures, including checkout, calibration, alignment, scheduled removal and replacement instructions, and associated checklists shall be validated against the system/equipment. The extent of validation is determined by the magnitude and complexity of the procedure being checked. However, malfunctions will not be introduced into the system or equipment for the purpose of validation unless specifically required for certification of procedural tasks or system tests.

    c. Only support equipment as approved by the government shall be used in the performance of validation. Simulation or substitution of support equipment must be approved by the procuring activity. It is the responsibility of the validator to submit his requests for government furnished equipment in sufficient time and quantities to support the validation effort.

    d. Validation shall constitute an integral part of the quality assurance program of the basic contract.

    e. The contractor is responsible for accomplishing the validating actions listed in his schedule in the manner prescribed in his procedures. Adequate notice shall be provided the government in order that a government representative may witness or participate, as appropriate.

    f. A TM is not considered validated until the following conditions have been fulfilled:

        (1) Contractor's engineering review has been completed.

        (2) TM procedures can be used to operate and maintain the system/equipment as stated.

        (3) Information reflects the configuration of the system/equipment and includes all engineering changes.

(4) Procedural instructions are readily understandable and adequate to perform all operation and maintenance functions.

(5) Sequence of operation and maintenance instructions are compatible with performance.

(6) Adequacy of data is checked to ensure that it supports approved maintenance and support plans.

g. Suitable records of all validation performed shall be maintained. These records shall indicate the affected manuals, weapon system, or component part number and/or serial number. The records shall be continuously maintained and be available for government review of justification or certification.

h. _Certification Report_. Upon completion of the validation tasks as identified by the validation plan, and at the time of manual submittal for procuring activity acceptance, the manual preparing activity shall deliver a document of certification attesting manual adequacy and accuracy and the satisfaction of the validation requirement.

2. _Verification_. Verification is the government's responsibility. The Central Management Office, MARCORSYSCOM (PSD), will coordinate and chair the verification effort and assign team leaders.

a. The verification team will be composed of:

(1) Chairperson (MARCORSYSCOM or designated representative).

(2) Technical Personnel (MARCORLOGBASES, Albany/ MARFORLANT/MARFORPAC/Marine Corps Schools) - Team Leaders.

(3) Target Users (FMF/Test Facilities).

b. A verification plan shall be prepared by the TM acquiring office and submitted to the contractor for comments. The plan shall include the requirement for low percent verification of all newly developed or revised TM's.

c. Verification may be simultaneously performed with validation in cases where time and equipment facilities availability do not permit separate validation, procedures are relatively simple, and the likelihood of errors is slight.

d. The verification process requires contractor assistance in addition to qualified personnel of the prescribed skill level from the operating command or agency to operate the equipment.

MARCORSYSCOM will indicate preliminary acceptance of the TM upon completion of the verification and incorporation of all changes resulting therefrom. Final acceptance will be made after receipt and review of final, camera-ready copy.

    e. Contractor support of verification shall consist of the following:

        (1) Assistance in the development of verification schedule and plan.

        (2) Recording and maintaining records of manual changes required as the result of, or associated with, verification; providing a record of verification to acquiring office.

        (3) When requested, provide assistance with verification tasks.

        (4) Making necessary corrections to discrepancies revealed during verification. Rewriting procedures, as required, within 48 hours of discovery of deficient material.

    f. In instances where a member of a field command, base, or school has been designated acting chairperson in lieu of MARCORSYSCOM, the assigned chairperson will certify to MARCORSYSCOM that the manual has been verified. Certification of completion of manual verification shall not be construed as acceptance of the manual.

    g. The verification team chairperson or acting chairperson shall maintain a master, marked-up copy of TM's being verified and shall prepare a record of verification comments, signed by team members, to be provided to the contractor and MARCORSYSCOM upon completion of verification effort.

APPENDIX D

SAMPLE TMCR

SUBJECT: TM

SCOPE: This TMCR presents requirements for development of the subject TM. The requirements specified herein constitute the TM tasks to be performed by the contractor and the resulting deliverables.

1.0 <u>APPLICABLE DOCUMENTS</u>

1.1 <u>Government Documents</u>. The following documents, of the issue in effect on the date of invitation for bids or request for proposal, form a part of this TMCR to the extent covered herein.

MIL-M-38784 *	Manuals, Technical: General Style and Format Requirements
MIL-M-85337 *	Manuals, Technical: Quality Assurance Program; Requirements for
MIL-STD-1840	Automated Interchange of Technical Information
MIL-M-28001	Markup Requirements and Generic Style Specification for Electronic Printed Output and Exchange of Text
MIL-R-28002	Military Specification, Raster Graphics Representation in Binary Format, Requirements for
MIL-P-28999	Publications, Technical, Instruction Type: Preparation of

*   Specifications to be used only if accompanied by request for waiver and justification for use.

2.0 <u>REQUIREMENTS</u>. In the event of conflict between the requirements of this TMCR, and the documents referenced herein, the requirements of the TMCR shall take precedence.

2.1 <u>TM QA Data</u>

2.1.1 <u>QA Program Plan</u>. The Contractor shall prepare a QA Program Plan that describes the scope and approach of the QA Program. The plan shall reflect the requirements of section 3.0 of this TMCR and include the following:

a. Organization. Contractor's QA organization and its functional relationship to the TM development and production organization(s). The authority, autonomy, and responsibilities of the QA organization.

b. Quality reviews. Contractor QA methods of monitoring and reviewing the processes for TM development and production.

c. Quality records. Quality-related records generated by TM development and production processes and by the contractor's QA reviews.

d. Corrective action. Contractor methods for ensuring that corrective and preventive actions are properly implemented and effective.

e. Data base control. Contractor control of the data base.

f. Control of subcontractors and vendors. Methods used by the contractor to ensure quality TM's from subcontractors and vendors.

2.1.2 TM Validation/Verification Plan. This plan shall reflect the requirements of section 4.0 of this TMCR and reflect compatibility with the overall maintenance and support plan, and indicate the scope of the validation effort. When so specified, the plan shall include recommendations for verification support.

2.1.2.1 Validation Plan. The plan shall consist of the following elements:

a. Manuals shall be identified in sufficient detail to permit rapid identification of material to be validated and verified.

b. Procedural methods of validation shall be identified in sufficient detail to assure the delivery of complete and accurate TM's. These procedures shall permit the performance of validating tasks in an environment which closely duplicates service conditions.

c. A planned program shall be scheduled that will ensure timely completion of validation and verification to meet scheduled manual deliveries.

d. The plan shall identify the cognizant preparing activity, organization, and personnel responsible for accomplishing the validation effort.

e. The plan shall identify site locations, kit requirements, facilities, and equipment required during validation effort.

f. The plan shall show a system of record keeping to be established which will fully document the validation effort, including method to be used to correct errors.

2.1.3 Validation Certification Report. Upon completion of the tasks as identified by the validation plan, and at the time of manual submittal for procuring activity acceptance, the manual preparing activity shall deliver a document of certification, attesting to the adequacy and accuracy of the TM and the satisfaction of the validation requirement. Individual validation certification reports shall be prepared for each TM validated by the contractor.

2.2 Manuals Technical: Preparation Instructions. An operation and maintenance manual shall be developed using LSA generated information as a data base. The manual shall be divided into two separate books and designated as follows: Operational and Organizational Maintenance (-12) and Intermediate Maintenance (-34). Refer to paragraph 2.2.3.1 for content organization of manuals.

2.2.1 Manuscript/Draft Copy. The manuscript shall be complete with front matter, text, tables, and illustrations. Included shall be corrections resulting from IPR's and validation, as applicable.

2.2.2 Format and Style. Preparation shall conform to the format and style in accordance with MIL-M-38784* with the exception that decimal numbering for paragraphs will not be used and the manual will be printed single column.

2.2.2.1 Cover and Title Page. The following distribution statement will be printed on the front cover of all unclassified manuals. The statement shall be centered, one half inch below the Marine Corps Seal in 0.09 inch type.

THIS PUBLICATION IS REQUIRED FOR OFFICIAL USE OR FOR ADMINISTRATIVE OR OPERATIONAL PURPOSES. DISTRIBUTION IS LIMITED TO U.S. GOVERNMENT AGENCIES ONLY. OTHER REQUESTS FOR THIS DOCUMENT MUST BE REFERRED TO: COMMANDANT OF THE MARINE CORPS (ARD-E), WASHINGTON, D.C. 20380-0001.

2.2.2.2 Destruction Notice. The following destruction notice will be printed two line spaces beneath the above distribution statement in 0.09 inch type.

DESTRUCTION NOTICE - FOR UNCLASSIFIED, LIMITED DOCUMENTS, DESTROY BY ANY METHOD THAT WILL PREVENT DISCLOSURE OF CONTENTS OR RECONSTRUCTION OF THE DOCUMENTS.

2.2.2.3 <u>Use Statement.</u> The statement "FOR OFFICIAL USE ONLY" shall appear in 0.20 inch type, 0.125 inch below the bottom horizontal-rule line, centered.

2.2.2.4 <u>Publication Number</u>. The publication shall be assigned a TM identification number. The number shall be placed on the cover(s) and shall be on all pages of the manual in the same type size as the basic manual. The number shall be assigned by MARCORSYSCOM (PSD).

2.2.2.5 <u>Photographs/Line Drawings</u>. Line drawings shall be prepared in lieu of photographs (half tones).

 * Use only if waiver for specification approved.

2.2.2.6 <u>Publication Date</u>. Until the camera-ready copy is produced, the publication date shall be the Copy Freeze Date which is an engineering cutoff date established by the procuring activity. No hardware changes will be incorporated into the publication after the Copy Freeze Date. The publication date shall be shown on the front cover only.

2.2.3 <u>Technical Content</u>. The TM shall conform to MIL-M-15071H* for technical content, with the following exceptions:

Page 3 Level of Writing, paragraph 3.3(c), add the word "no" between the words having and previous.

Page 5 Paragraph 3.4.2.1.1, Cover and Title Page. No requirement for Title Page for the Marine Corps.

Page 5 Paragraph 3.4.2.1.4, Approval and Procurement Record page (types I and III only). This requirement is deleted.

Page 6 Paragraph 3.4.6, User Activity Comment Sheets; not required.

Page 7 Paragraph 3.5.2, Chapters. Installation Chapter shall always be Chapter 2 in the TM. The requirement for Chapter 7 is deleted.

Page 8 Paragraph 3.5.3.6. First sentence applicable only.

Page 9 Paragraph 3.5.3.7. Deleted.

Page 11 Paragraph 3.5.4.4.1(g). Reference to the Standard Log Sheet. The requirement for this paragraph is deleted.

Page 16 Paragraph 3.5.6.3(a), (f), (h), and (i). Preventive Maintenance Procedures. The requirements of these subparagraphs are deleted.

Page 16 Paragraph 3.5.6.4(d). The minimum rating of the technician expected to perform the task. This requirement is deleted.

Page 25 Paragraph 3.5.7.2.12.2, Troubleshooting-Maintenance Dependency-Matrix Chart. The requirements of this paragraph are deleted.

Page 26 Paragraph 3.5.9, Chapter 7, Parts List. The requirements of this paragraph are deleted.

* Use specification only if waiver for use is granted.

Page 32 Paragraph 3.5.10.9(a) and (c). Installation Check-out. The requirements of these subparagraphs are deleted.

Page 44 Paragraph 3.7.6, Foldout Pages. This paragraph is changed to read "All foldout illustrations shall be located at the rear of the book in which they occur, provided such location does not reduce the clarity of the text."

Page 45 Paragraph 3.7.8, Paragraph numbering is amended. Decimal numbering will not be used.

Page 45 Paragraph 3.8(f) is deleted.

2.2.3.1 Equipment Manuals Organization. When the TM is divided into two levels, it shall be organized as follows:

-12 Operation and Organizational Maintenance:

Chapter 1 - General Information and Safety Precautions
Chapter 2 - Installation
Chapter 3 - Operation
Chapter 4 - Functional Description (Paragraph 3.5.5 - 3.5.5.2.5.1, as applicable)
Chapter 5 - Scheduled Maintenance (PMCS)
Chapter 6 - Troubleshooting (Limited)
Chapter 7 - Corrective Maintenance

-34 Intermediate Maintenance:

Chapter 1 - General Information and Safety Precautions
Chapter 2 - Functional Description/Theory of Operation
Chapter 3 - Scheduled Maintenance (if applicable)
Chapter 4 - Troubleshooting
Chapter 5 - Corrective Maintenance

2.2.4 Reproducible Copy and Integrally Related Art. Manuscripts having corrections resulting from IPR's and verification, as

applicable, shall be incorporated. The material shall be prepared legible and usable at the most economical cost, considering
initial and follow-on costs, such as reproduction, printing,
handling, filing, storing, and equipment, and any combination
thereof. Electric accounting machines, computers, punched cards,
and tapes may be used for preparing text.

2.2.5 _Digital Data_. In addition to hard copy manuals, the contractor shall provide digitized data in an electronic media
(excluding optical) in a non-proprietary format. MIL-STD-1840
shall be used for the development and delivery of electronic
media. The deliverable shall be an electronic TM consisting of
SGML tagged files for the entire text of the TM. The deliverable
shall be a processible data file composed of one set of files for
textual data and one set of files for graphics (illustrations).

2.2.5.1 _Text_. The text file shall be tagged in accordance with
MIL-M-28001. File structure shall consist of a header record
followed by the tagged data record, as specified by MIL-STD-1840.

2.2.5.2 _Final Deliverables_. Final deliverable shall consist of
a camera-ready copy of the TM and digital media. In addition,
the digitized deliverable shall be prepared in accordance with
the TMCR tailored to the specific program and delivered in accordance with the CDRL.

3.0 _QUALITY ASSURANCE PROVISIONS_

3.1 _TM QUALITY ASSURANCE PROGRAM_. The contractor shall document
and maintain a TM QA program to the extent necessary to assure
that the TM's procured under this contract accurately and adequately reflect the production equipment. The contractor shall
conduct TM quality assurance program planning. The QA planning
effort shall address support of conferences, IPR's, and TM verification. The contractor shall conduct TM validation and submit
certification thereof to the government in accordance with the
CDRL.

3.1.1 _IPR_. IPR's may be requested by the government to provide
for coordinated monitoring of TM preparation by the contractor
and the government. The contractor shall support IPR's and
provide access to TM materials, intermediate products, and final
products. The IPR's shall include evaluation of:

    a. Source data

    b. TM plan/outlines

    c. Presentation methods

    d. Modes of preparation

e. TMCR compliance

f. Complete documentation (text and artwork)

3.1.1.1 <u>Scheduling IPR's</u>. IPR's shall be held at the contractor's or designated government facility. The contractor shall submit an IPR schedule for review during the initial Guidance Conference, if applicable. IPR's will be held at various stages of TM development prior to preparation of final reproducible copy. The contractor may request IPR's when assistance or clarification is desired. The government may require and the contractor may request additional IPR's irrespective of the schedule.

3.1.1.2 <u>IPR Records</u>. The contractor shall act as recorder and record decisions/discrepancies resulting from or associated with IPR's.

3.1.1.3 <u>Disposition of IPR Findings</u>. Discrepancies and/or deficiencies found as the result of an IPR shall be corrected prior to certification and acceptance of the TM.

3.1.2 <u>Validation</u>. Validation is a contractor QA responsibility accomplished on all TM's, changes, and revisions thereto. Validation shall not be considered complete until the following conditions have been fulfilled:

a. Contractor's engineering technical review has been completed.

b. Information reflects configuration of the system/ equipment and includes all engineering changes.

c. Procedural instructions are readily understandable by the intended user and adequate to perform all operations and maintenance functions.

d. Adequacy of data is checked to ensure that it supports the approved maintenance and support plan.

e. Hardware of the proper configuration is available for the validation effort.

3.1.2.1 Validation Performance. Theory and principles of operation, system/component description, services codes, schematic, and wiring data shall be validated against engineering source data. Operating and maintenance procedures, including checkout, alignment, scheduled removal and replacement instructions, and associated checklists shall be validated against the system/ equipment by actual demonstration. Malfunctions will not be introduced into the system or equipment for the purpose of validation unless specifically required for clarification of procedural tasks or system tests.

3.1.2.2 <u>Support Equipment</u>. Government-approved support equipment shall be used in the performance of validation. Simulation or substitution of support equipment must be approved by the government. It is the responsibility of the contractor to submit requests for government furnished equipment to support the validation effort.

3.1.2.3 <u>Validation Records</u>. Records of all validations performed shall be maintained. These records shall indicate the affected manuals, systems, or component part number and/or serial number. The records shall be maintained and be available for government review.

3.1.2.4 <u>Disposition of Validated Data</u>. Corrections and significant comments resulting from validation shall be incorporated prior to the certification and acceptance of the TM.

3.1.2.5 <u>Validation Certification</u>. The contractor shall submit validation certification attesting to the TM adequacy and accuracy in accordance with the TMCR. The certificate shall be signed by authorized contractor representatives.

3.2 <u>Contractor Surveillance</u>. The contractor shall maintain the QA program in accordance with the contractor's TM QA Program Plan. Contractor surveillance shall be performed on a continuing basis to ensure compliance with his quality program plans, this TMCR, and the contract.

3.3 <u>Government Surveillance</u>. The government may conduct a Guidance and Quality Planning Conference and Quality Program Review throughout the term of the contract to ensure compliance with the TM QA Program Plan, this TMCR, the contract, and the production of a quality product.

4.0 <u>PACKAGING AND DELIVERY</u>

4.1 <u>Package Marking</u>. In addition to sender and addressee information, the exterior of each package shall bear the following:

    a. Publication number

    b. Contract or purchase order number

    c. Type of material enclosed

    d. Number of containers in the shipment

4.2 <u>Packing List</u>. A copy of the letter of transmittal or the packing list shall be placed inside the package. When a shipment consists of several packages, the letter of transmittal or packing list shall be enclosed in the first package and shall identify the material that was wrapped in each package.

4.3 <u>Manual, Technical</u>

4.3.1 <u>Manuscript Copy for Review</u>. Manuscript copies shall be wrapped separately and packaged flat in cartons. Final size illustrations shall be included in the manuscript. Foldouts shall be folded as necessary to fit the bound manuscript. Maximum thickness of bound matter shall be three inches, not including covers. If the number of foldouts is enough to cause a substantial difference in the thickness of the manuscript on the binding edge, spacers shall be added to equalize the two sides of the manuscript. The manuscript shall be bound with posts or inserted in three-ring binders. Elaborate containers shall not be used. Packaging must protect the manuscript so that it cannot shift within the container.

4.3.2 <u>Reproducible Copy and Integrally Related Art</u>. The reproducible (camera-ready) copy shall be packaged flat and double-packaged. Artwork shall not be folded or rolled. The interior material shall be waterproof and free of any chemical substance that would discolor or otherwise render the reproducible copy useless. The exterior package shall be a standard commercial carton at least equal to interstate commerce standards and of sufficient strength to provide for safety and safe delivery, and to protect the camera-ready copy against damage during shipping.

5.0 <u>DELIVERABLES</u>

5.1 <u>TM Book Plan and Outlines</u>. A TM book plan and outlines to show planned composition of the manuals to be developed and delivered to the government 60 DAC.

5.2 <u>Draft Manual</u>. The Contractor shall submit draft manuals 30 days after FAT for government review/approval. Government requires 60 days for review.

5.3 <u>Reproducible</u>. One set of hard copy reproducibles shall be provided to the Commander, Marine Corps Systems Command, (Code PSD), 60 days after receipt of government comments. Government requires 30 days for review/approval. Government comments shall be incorporated prior to delivery of reproducibles.

5.4 <u>Digitized Data.</u> Digitized data shall be delivered on magnetic tape in accordance with paragraph 2.2.5 and be provided concurrent with delivery of hard copy reproducibles.

APPENDIX E

DEFINITIONS AND TYPES OF IETM'S AND ETM'S

1. <u>Five Classes of Automated TM Systems</u>. The five classes of systems are listed and described in more detail below.

<u>Class 1</u>. Page-Image Display Systems - Systems of Digitized Page Images intended for Full-Page Display using an Intelligent Index to the page images for user interaction (e.g., Navy ATIS).

<u>Class 2</u>. Hypertext Display of Page-Oriented Documents - Systems for Interactive Display of ASCII encoded, Page-Oriented Documents using Hypertext tagging added to SGML tagged document files.

<u>Class 3</u>. Hypertext ETM's - Systems for Interactive Display of Technical Information which is marked-up (i.e., SGML tagged) in accordance with MIL-D-87269 (Data Base, Revisable: Inter-active Electronic TM's, for the Support of), but based on a linear document file, and displayed in accordance with MIL-M-87268 (Manuals, Interactive Electronic Technical: General Content, Style, Format, and User-Interaction Requirements).

<u>Class 4</u>. Data-Base Oriented IETM's - Systems for Interactive Electronic Display of TM Material specifically authored in a data base form and subsequently packaged for Interactive Presentation in accordance with the IETM Specifications (MIL-M-87268, MIL-D-87269, and MIL-Q-87270 QA Program: Interactive Electronic TM's and Associated Technical Information; Requirements for).

<u>Class 5</u>. Integrated Process IETM's - Systems for Interactive Presentation of TM's integrated with other processes including Expert-System rules for the display of information designed to be displayed by those rules or processes.

a. Each of these classes has benefits over the current paper TM systems and the degree of benefit increases with each higher class. The first class can be built at relatively low cost using scanned images or Postscript encodings of the present inventory of paper TM's (i.e., legacy data) and include systems in which benefits are focused on eliminating problems with the excessive space and weight requirements of paper manuals and the problems of printing paper and maintaining change-page updates. The second class is designed to add the benefits of an interactive presentation to documents being developed using a conventional publication system with the format and content developed according to existing TM specifications.

b. Class 3 is the class in which the TM authorizing organization has an opportunity to augment and convert an existing manual into an IETM form in order to increase technician performance, in addition to providing the benefits achieved by eliminating paper. Classes 4 and 5 take best advantage of the electronic media because they are specifically authored and maintained for those media. Class 5 can only be loosely defined at this time. Its inclusion in the classification scheme is intended to anticipate various future integrated concepts, which can be demonstrated to achieve performance results better than the other classes of automated TM Presentation systems. Class 5 approaches are expected to achieve better performance as well as increase the scope of the IETM by integrating additional applications such as just-in-time training system, an active expert advice system, or an other computational diagnostic process performed at display time to enhance the presentation of information to the user.

2. Page Image Display Systems. Class 1 systems employ a full page encoding of a document (e.g., CCITT Group 4 Fax compression or Postscript page-description language) and include those being developed for the Navy ATIS as well as the TMPODS. The image storage and display technology used is fully developed and in use on Navy ships. The electronic-display version of this class is one in which a user views a full-page image on a screen with page-turning and limited look-up capability using an intelligent index. These systems have interactive features to the extent possible without changing the page integrity of the data. The basic TM's which are handled by Class 1 systems are not authored for electronic display.

3. Hypertext Display of Page-Oriented Documents. Class 2 systems are those specifically designed to retrofit existing page-oriented TM's into an electronic retrieval and display capability. For many of these applications, a service bureau digitizes the existing page images in a variety of ways and adds indexing and cross-referencing information in the best manner it can, but without (in general) the involvement of the original authoring contractor. Other applications involve on-line document viewers, typically associated with the automated publishing system used to prepare the original document. These electronic versions of the documents are not formally revalidated and as such cannot be extensively modified. Class 2 systems are represented by the emerging SGML-Viewers now coming onto the market.

4. Hypertext IETM's. Class 3 systems are those designed to display conventionally specified TM's originally intended for printing in paper form but which have been converted to be displayed in an IETM format. The critical criteria to call a tagged document Class 3 is to require SGML tagging be in

conformance with a MIL-D-87269 Document Type Definition, and to which the MIL-D-87269 interaction tagged attributes have been added to the document file to facilitate interactive presentation. Class 3 systems represent a bridge capability to make current document files capable of being converted for electronic display with most of the features of Class 4 Systems (i.e., IETM Data-Base Systems).

5. <u>Data-Base Oriented Interactive Electronic TM's</u>. Class 4 systems (IETM) are those for which the TM data was specifically authored into a data base form which contains the necessary data elements and attributes required for a computer to display the data in an interactive presentation. In this class the authoring organization initially prepares a relational or object-oriented data base which contains the IETM data elements, their attributes and links which are later extracted, compiled, and formatted to create a "View-Package" of the data base which can be processed for display by a electronic display system such as a portable maintenance aid. This class is specifically that for which requirements have been promulgated in the series of DoD IETM Specifications. It is most applicable to a major new weapons systems or a major rewrite of an existing TM suite.

6. <u>Integrated Process Interactive Electronic TM's</u>

   a. Class 5 systems will differ from the others in that they will provide computer programs or expert-system processes to the user as well as the IETM information. These programs will provide intelligent information to the user such as the Expert-System processes to guide the user in accessing maintenance data, in performing diagnosis and trouble-shooting, or in undergoing Computer-Based Training Procedures. These procedures will involve interactive dialogue initiated by the Expert-System program, which will supplement the user-initiated controls provided by a Class 4 capability in viewing the IETM information.

   b. Systems of the Class 5 type exist and can be demonstrated at this time but, in general, are proprietary in implementation and, typically, involve state-of-the-art technology and are somewhat experimental in nature. They are, however, very suited to operating in a system which is based on a carefully constructed database of fixed preauthored information, as in Class 4 IETM data base, and can be designed to be a natural extension of such an IETM data base. As such, all of the IETM specifications can apply to Class 5 data deliverables and the presentation system. The actual additional computational process would have to be separately specified. Class 5 databases include software products which are integrated in with the IETM (e.g., computational processes, or expert system rules) as well as authored Technical Information as the delivered products.

7. <u>Interrelationship between the Five Classes of Automated TM Systems</u>. Essential to the development of this classification system is the concept that the criteria which most uniquely distinguish these systems are not those which establish the characteristics of the user system or of the electronic presentation, but those involved in establishing the structure and format of the underlying data and the operations needed to prepare that data and process it into displayable TM form. At the user-presentation level, Classes 2 through 5 can show similar features. However, Class 1 and 2 are after-the-fact preparation systems while Classes 3, 4, and 5 involve TM's prepared by the authoring organization. Classes 1, 2, and 3 involve encoding a linear document with its existing page structure; Classes 4 and 5 employ the use of information extracted from a random-access data base and compiled into a form optimized for interactive screen presentation and from which there is no easy method to replicate paper-page images. Class 5 is distinct in that it involves other run-time software as part of the integrated delivered product.

E-4

THE MARINE CORPS TECHNICAL PUBLICATIONS SYSTEM

DoD Classes of Electronic TM's

	Class 0 - Non-electronically indexed Page Images [Not an ETM]	Class 1 - Electronically Indexed Page Images	Class 2 - Electronic Scrolling Documents	Class 3 - Linearly Structured IETMs	Class 4 - Hierarchically Structured IETMs	Class 5 - Integrated Data Base IETIS
DISPLAY	Printed Pages; Includes Microform Imaging; Full Page Viewing	View full page image; Preserves page integrity of printed page; Page-turner NEXT function; Intelligent index for user access to page images	Primary display is scrolling text window; Hot-Spot access (Hyper-Links) to other text or graphics; User selectable call to i.e., "launch") another process (e.g., animation, video); Text is minimally formatted for display window (Scrolling, Wordwrap, style sheet for fonts); User selection and navigation aids (Key-word search, On-line indexes)	Interaction through dialog boxes; Text and graphics simultaneously displayed in separate windows when keyed together; Interaction functions per MIL-M-87268 to the extent possible; View smaller logical blocks of text - Less use of scrolling text (than Class 2)	Interaction through Dialog Boxes with user prompts; Text and graphics simultaneously displayed in separate windows when keyed together; Interaction functions per MIL-M-87268; View smaller logical blocks of text; Very limited use of scrolling text (much less than Class 3)	Multi-function display section; Same as Class 4 when in ITEM function; Interactive electronic display per MIL-M-87268; Expert system to allow same display session and viewing system to assist in simultaneous access to many differing functions such as troubleshooting, inventory status or parts, and training
DATA FORMAT	Film (negs or microform); WP or Comp System Formats; SGML Files; MIL-R-28002; Page Description Language; Generic: Any format for page image	Bit Map (Raster) with indexing information and headers; Indexing and header files (MIL-29532 for Navy); MIL-R-28002 or Postscript for Pages; Generic: Format associated with COTS imaging systems applications for pages, indexing, and headers	Text - ASCII; Graphics - whatever graphics viewer will support - typically BMP or CALS; Can be SGML tagged with no page breaks (i.e., SGML browser); Access and indexing information typically COTS retrieval software and Hypertext browser; Generic: Can use COTS format of Hypertext browser used	Linear ASCII text with SGML tags; SGML tagged document but with "content tags" vs. "document format tags"; MIL-D-87269 used to the maximum extent possible; Generic: Use of SGML content tags equivalent to MIL-D-87269 tags	Fully attributed data-base elements described in MIL-D-87269; MIL-D-87269 content tags with full conformance to Generic Level Object Outlines (Architectural Forms); Authored directly to date base specifically for interactive electronic output; Data managed by Data Base Management System (too complex otherwise); Interactive features authored in original creation vice added later; Generic: COTS equivalent to MIL-D-87269 for data definition and tags	IETM information integrated at date-level with other application information; Does not use separate data bases for other application data (e.g. training, parts inventory); Identical to Class 4 (IETM) standards for IETM application date per MIL-D-87269; Includes coding for Expert System Rules and AI software when used; Generic: COTS equivalent to MIL-D-87269 for data definition and tags
FUNCTIONALITY	Print Page(s); View page w/o intelligent index access	Access pages via intelligent index and/or header information; View page images on full-page display (or via pen and zoom on smaller display); Limited use of hot spots on page to reference another page; Utility limited to library and reference use	Browse through scrolling information; User selection of graphics or hot spot reference to additional text; Hot-Spots and Cross References typically added after original authoring	Dialog-driven interaction; Logical display of information in accordance with content; Logical NEXT and BACK function; Useful as Interactive Maintenance Aid; User-selectable cross references and indexes; Context-specific help available	Dialog-driven interaction; Logical display of information in accordance with content; Logical NEXT and BACK function; Useful as Interactive Maintenance Aid; User-selectable cross references and indexes; Context-specific help available	A single viewing system for simultaneous access to multiple information sources; Class 4 standards for IETM application; Expert System to assist in NEXT function base on information gathered during session

APPENDIX F

IROAN DEPOT MAINTENANCE MANUALS

The following paragraphs are intended to provide guidance for the development of the IROAN portion of the depot maintenance manual. As a minimum, the following areas should be addressed:

a. The Preshop Analysis Checklist shall be prepared to contain visual external inspections, test, and analysis maintenance actions required of the end item/assembly/subassembly to determine the extent of the repair operations necessary to bring the equipment to a serviceable condition as stated by the depot maintenance manual.

b. In-process inspection requirements shall be provided where they are applicable in the maintenance tasks (removal, disassembly, cleaning, and repair) to include inspection procedures with accept/reject criteria for all items with critical characteristics/wear limits/tolerances. Accept/reject information shall be sufficient to determine that new, repaired, and used components conforms to wear limits and tolerances established by the depot maintenance manual.

c. Disassembly Instructions shall be given in proper sequence with instructions for inspection inserted where they should be performed. Disassembly performed, including thorough visual and mechanical inspection, shall not be limited to the removal and separation of mechanical items such as cover plates, gears, and electronic chassis. When applicable, instructions shall be included for checking and recording gear wear patterns and back checking, or recording and tagging defective parts with reasons for rejection.

d. Final Assembly Testing - The techniques and methods required to ensure the satisfactory performance of the item shall be described in detail. These shall include a description of inspections and tests of functional, dimensional, and any other characteristic required to ensure that the item has been adequately overhauled per the inspection checklist or depot maintenance. If the equipment requires a run-in or burn-in test, compliance instructions shall be incorporated. Charts shall be included in the test instruction showing variations in parameters at different operating conditions. A checklist indicating each inspection required shall be included.

APPENDIX G

DISTRIBUTION AND PCN'S

1. <u>Distribution Determination.</u> The requirements for distri-
bution of a technical publication is jointly determined by the
Program Manager and the Central Management Office, MARCORSYSCOM
(PSD).

2. <u>Assignment of PCN's.</u> MARCORSYSCOM (PSD) as the sponsor of
all Marine Corps technical publications, assigns PCN's, and
enters numbers assigned into the MCPDS. The PCN performs two
functions: replaces the generic code previously used to denote
the distribution on any specific publication and acts as the
stock number for requisitioning purposes. Using MCPDS, managers
and users may, by PCN identification, obtain any information
required on any specific publication; e.g., requisition, view
date of publication, associated identification numbers, sponsor
code, short or long title, classification status, and distribution.